THE OFFICIAL
WEST HAM UNITED
ANNUAL 2013

Written by Rob Pritchard

Design by Lucy Boyd

A Grange Publication

© 2012. Published by Grange Communications Ltd., Edinburgh, under licence from West Ham United Football Club. Printed in the EU.

Photographs © West Ham United Football Club

ISBN no. 978-1-908925-17-6

£7.99

CONTENTS

WEST HAM UNITED OFFICIAL ANNUAL 2013

THIS BOOK BELONGS TO:	
MY AGE:	
MY SCHOOL:	
MY FOOTBALL TEAM:	
MY POSITION:	
MY FAVOURITE WEST HAM UNITED PLAYER:	
MY PREDICTION OF WHERE WEST HAM UNITED WILL FINISH IN THE BARCLAYS PREMIER LEAGUE:	

Welcome to the Official West Ham United Annual 2013!

Well, what a year 2012 was for West Ham United!

We ended last season by celebrating promotion back to the Barclays Premier League after a thrilling npower Championship Play-Off final victory over Blackpool at Wembley.

The 2011/12 season was long, tough but ultimately successful, highlighted by so many outstanding individual and team performances and a club record 13 away league victories.

Players like our captain Kevin Nolan, Ricardo Vaz Te and Carlton Cole and home-grown heroes like Mark Noble, Jack Collison and James Tomkins all stepped up to the mark when it really mattered – but we would not have achieved anything without your amazing support.

One of the true pleasures of my first year in charge of this great football club was meeting so many of you – the fans who are the beating heart of West Ham United.

Your passion, pride and commitment willed us on to promotion and I was personally delighted to see so many smiling faces at Wembley back in May.

Since then, the hard work has continued as we prepared and began life back in the Barclays Premier League – the biggest, best and toughest division in the world.

While east London celebrated the London 2012 Olympic Games, we left no stone unturned in our quest to ensure West Ham continue to dine at the top table of English football for many, many years to come.

As the Board have rightly said, this truly is Moore than a Football Club.

We have an amazing fan base, a first-team squad to be proud of and one of the best Academies in the world – there is so much to be proud of at West Ham United.

Everything we do at West Ham United is for you. We look to entertain and win every time we play and there is no doubt the tremendous backing you provide gives us a massive lift whenever the players take to the pitch.

We will never take your support for granted and the players will make sure that they reward your support with 100 per cent effort and commitment.

This is a club with a great history and traditions and, I hope, an even greater future.

Come on you Irons!

KEVIN NOLAN

Message from the Captain

Hello everyone and welcome to the Official West Ham United Annual 2013.

I would like to start by saying 'Thank you' to each and every one of you for your absolutely amazing support over the past year.

Without your loyalty and commitment, we would not have been able to achieve everything we did in 2012 – most notably promotion back to the Barclays Premier League and a club record of 13 away league wins in a season.

Everywhere we went during the season, you sang longer and louder than the opposition, encouraging us on to victory and, ultimately, a fantastic success at Wembley which you all thoroughly deserved.

I am sure that same support will serve us well in the Barclays Premier League as we seek to consolidate our place in the biggest and best league in the world.

We know it will not be easy, but I can assure you that each and every one of us will be working harder than ever before to ensure you have more goals and wins to enjoy between now and the end of the season.

I will close by wishing you and your families a very Merry Christmas and a Happy and Healthy New Year.

Come on you Irons!

Kevin Nolan

A concise look back on the history of the Hammers

West Ham United was founded in 1895 as Thames Ironworks FC before being reformed in 1900. In 1904 the club relocated to their current Boleyn Ground stadium in Upton Park.

After initially competing in the Southern League and Western League, West Ham joined the Football League in 1919. Four years later, the Hammers celebrated the twin achievements of gaining promotion to Division One and reaching the first-ever Wembley FA Cup final, where they were beaten by Bolton Wanderers.

The 1920s and early 1930s were the domain of the Club's greatest-ever goalscorer, Vic Watson, who bagged an amazing 326 goals in claret and blue.

In 1940 the team returned to Wembley and won the inaugural Football League War Cup, defeating Blackburn Rovers at Wembley thanks to Sam Small's first-half winner.

West Ham have continued to be regular visitors to the Home of Football, winning the FA Cup in 1964, 1975 and 1980 and the European Cup Winners' Cup in 1965, defeating German side TSV 1860 Munich 2-0 in the final.

The Hammers have also reached Wembley in the League Cup, holding Liverpool to a draw in 1981 before being beaten in a replay at Villa Park.

The Club finished as runners-up to West Bromwich Albion in the same competition in 1966 – the same year in which Bobby Moore, Geoff Hurst and Martin Peters led England to FIFA World Cup glory.

In continental competition, aside from their 1965 triumph, the Hammers reached the final of the European Cup Winners' Cup again in 1976, losing to Belgian club RSC Anderlecht, and won the UEFA Intertoto Cup in 1999.

HONOURS

European Cup Winners Cup
Winners – 1965
Runners-up – 1976

FA Cup
Winners – 1964, 1975, 1980
Runners-up – 1923, 2006

League Cup
Runners-up – 1966, 1981

UEFA Intertoto Cup
Winners – 1999

Football League Championship Play-Off
Winners – 2005, 2012
Runners-up – 2004

Football League Championship
(Previously Division One and Division Two)
Winners – 1957/58, 1980/81
Runners-up – 1922/23, 1990/91, 1991/92

Football League War Cup
Winners – 1940

Charity Shield
Winners – 1964 (shared with Liverpool)

FA Youth Cup
Winners – 1963, 1981, 1999
Runners-up – 1957, 1959, 1975, 1996

In terms of league position, West Ham's highest-ever finish was the third place achieved by John Lyall's squad in 1985/86.

Unfortunately for the club, those past glories meant nothing as they were relegated from the Premier League after a six-year stay in the top-flight in May 2011.

Just 12 months later, however, Sam Allardyce led West Ham back to where they belong in the Barclays Premier League following a record-breaking season that saw them promoted via the Championship Play-Offs.

Hammer of the Year

Mark Noble was crowned 2011/12 Hammer of the Year

The midfielder capped a superb promotion season by scooping the prestigious award – sponsored by Alpari (UK) – at West Ham United's fourth annual Awards Dinner at the London Hilton on Park Lane. Alpari (UK) COO David Stuart was on hand to present Noble with his award.

Twice runner-up, Noble was rewarded for his outstanding performances over the past nine months by edging James Tomkins into second place after more than 10,000 votes were cast by West Ham supporters. Robert Green came in third and Kevin Nolan fourth.

"It does sound really nice to be named Hammer of the Year, to be honest!" said a delighted Noble. "I have been runner-up a few times so it is just nice to win one.

"I just want us to get back in the Premier League – that's my aim and I've just tried my best to help my club to do that. We've got three more games left and hopefully we can do it."

Lifelong Hammers Noble joins an elite band of winners that includes greats such as Bobby Moore, Geoff Hurst, Billy Bonds, Trevor Brooking and Scott Parker.

Homegrown hero Noble enjoyed a fantastic season in claret and blue, scoring a career-high nine goals and chalking up a club-best 48 npower Championship and Play-Off appearances and nine assists.

The No 16 also picked up the Best Individual Performance award for his two-goal show in the home victory over Nottingham Forest in January 2012 and, along with James Tomkins, was voted into the npower Championship Team of the Year by his fellow professionals.

Other winners at the Awards Dinner included Ricardo Vaz Te, who won Best Signing and Best Goal, Save of the Season winner Robert Green, Players' Player of the Year George McCartney, Young Hammer of the Year Dan Potts and Academy Player of the Year Rob Hall.

Carlton Cole finished as Top Goalscorer for the fourth consecutive season, while Best Team Performance award went to the side that won 4-1 at Blackpool in February 2012.

WEST HAM UNITED

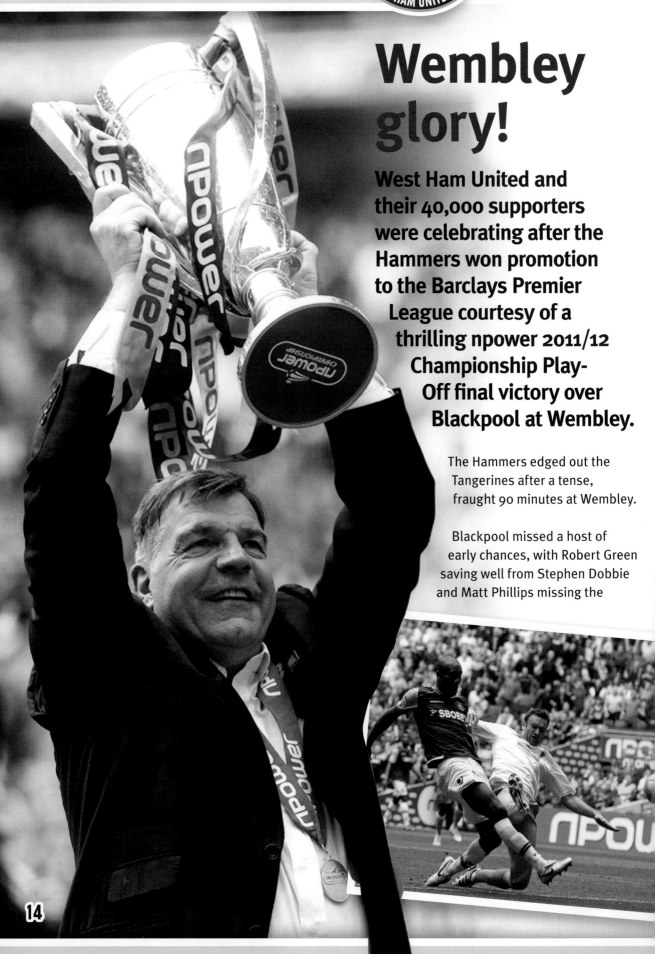

Wembley glory!

West Ham United and their 40,000 supporters were celebrating after the Hammers won promotion to the Barclays Premier League courtesy of a thrilling npower 2011/12 Championship Play-Off final victory over Blackpool at Wembley.

The Hammers edged out the Tangerines after a tense, fraught 90 minutes at Wembley.

Blackpool missed a host of early chances, with Robert Green saving well from Stephen Dobbie and Matt Phillips missing the target with two shots from the edge of the penalty area.

Having survived an early barrage from Ian Holloway's side, West Ham recovered to take the lead ten minutes before half-time when Carlton Cole lost his marker and latched on to Matt Taylor's diagonal pass before finishing past goalkeeper Matt Gilks.

Ricardo Vaz Te slid a shot wide a short time later and it looked like the Portuguese's effort would prove costly when Thomas Ince collected Phillips' pass before striking low past Green's right hand.

The closing half-hour saw Blackpool come on strong again, but West Ham recovered and hit the crossbar through captain Kevin Nolan.

Sam Allardyce's side snatched victory just as extra-time loomed large when Jack Collison sent Nolan clear down the left. The skipper looked up and crossed and when Cole's shot was saved by Gilks, Vaz Te was on hand to smash the ball into the roof of the net.

Moments later, the Hammers were celebrating as Howard Webb's final whistle signalled the club's welcome return to the top-flight at the first time of asking.

Show your support for West Ham United's claret and blue traditions by colouring in this image of striker Carlton Cole!

QUIZ

Spot the Difference

Can you spot the eight differences between these two images taken during West Ham United's pre-season match at Boreham Wood?

You can find the answers on page 60.

MEET the Manager and Backroom Staff

Sam Allardyce – Manager

Known universally as 'Big Sam', Dudley-born Sam Allardyce is one of the most experienced and respected managers in the English game. A fearsome centre-back as a player, Big Sam forged his managerial reputation during eight years in charge at Bolton Wanderers. The 58-year-old led West Ham United to promotion to the Barclays Premier League in his first season at the Boleyn Ground.

Sam Allardyce

Neil McDonald – Assistant Manager

Neil McDonald

Born in the same town, Wallsend, as former West Ham United midfielder Michael Carrick, Neil McDonald was a reliable full-back who enjoyed success with Newcastle United and Everton. Capped five times by England at Under-21 level, McDonald featured for The Toffees in the 1989 FA Cup final before acting as Sam Allardyce's No 2 at Bolton Wanderers and Blackburn Rovers.

Wally Downes – First-team Coach

Born in Hammersmith in west London, Wally Downes made his name as a member of the infamous 'Crazy Gang' during nine seasons as a professional with Wimbledon. The former midfielder, who turned 51 in June 2012, embarked on his coaching career with Crystal Palace and Reading, where he worked under Steve Coppell, before joining West Ham United in November 2010.

Wally Downes

Martyn Margetson – Goalkeeper Coach

Martyn Margetson

A former Wales international goalkeeper, Martyn Margetson enjoyed a successful 15-year playing career with Manchester City, Southend United, Huddersfield Town and Cardiff City. The West Neath-born stopper became the Bluebirds' goalkeeper coach while still a player in 2005 before taking the job up full-time. He became Wales' goalkeeper coach in January 2011.

Meet the
TEAM

WEST HAM UNITED

Born: 19 April 1975, Mikkeli, Finland

Position: Goalkeeper

Height: 1.91m

Former club: Bolton Wanderers

International: Finland (56 caps)

A consistent and vastly-experienced goalkeeper, Jussi Jaaskelainen joined West Ham United in the summer of 2012 after 15 seasons with Bolton Wanderers.

The 1.91m tall stopper made more than 500 appearances for the Trotters, helping the Lancashire club to gain promotion to the Premier League, twice qualify for the UEFA Cup and reach the League Cup final.

Capped 56 times by Finland and voted the country's Player of the Year in 2007, Jaaskelainen made his debut against Malta in 1998 before retiring from international football in October 2010.

1 JUSSI JAASKELAINEN

New Zealand international Winston Reid became a national hero when he headed in a late equaliser for the All Whites against Slovakia at the 2010 FIFA World Cup in South Africa.

Snapped up from Danish club FC Midtjylland shortly after that tournament, Reid recovered from a difficult first season in English football to play a huge part in West Ham United's promotion from the npower Championship in 2011/12.

The powerful centre-back ensured his status among Hammers supporters when he blasted in the winner in a 2-1 home win over rivals Millwall in February 2012.

Born: 3 July 1988, North Shore, New Zealand

Position: Centre-back

Height: 1.90m

Former club: FC Midtjylland

International: New Zealand (11 caps, 1 goal)

WINSTON REID 2

Born: 29 April 1981, Belfast, Northern Ireland

Position: Left-back

Height: 1.83m

Former club: Sunderland

International: Northern Ireland (34 caps, 1 goal)

Popular among his West Ham United team-mates and supporters alike, consistent left-back George McCartney is now in his second spell at the Boleyn Ground.

After a successful two-year spell between 2006 and 2008, the Northern Irishman returned to east London on loan in the summer of 2011.

A superb season saw McCartney score his second goal for the Club at Cardiff City in March 2012 and cap the campaign with promotion and the Players' Player of the Year award.

3 GEORGE McCARTNEY

West Ham United's captain led the Club to promotion from the npower Championship in his first season at the Boleyn Ground.

An inspiring figure on and off the pitch, Kevin Nolan enjoyed a successful career with Bolton Wanderers and Newcastle United prior to his move to London, chalking up more than 350 Premier League appearances and appearing in the UEFA Cup and League Cup final.

Renowned for his goalscoring, Nolan found the net on 13 occasions in 2011/12, including a vital header in the npower Championship Play-Off semi-final second leg against Cardiff City in May 2012.

Born: 24 June 1982, Liverpool, England

Position: Central midfield

Height: 1.83m

Former club: Newcastle United

International: England Under-21 (2 caps)

KEVIN NOLAN 4

Born: 29 March 1989, Basildon, England

Position: Centre-back

Height: 1.92m

Former club: Derby County (loan)

International: England Under-21 (10 caps)

A product of the Academy of Football, it is surely only a matter of time before James Tomkins emulates fellow graduates Bobby Moore and Rio Ferdinand by winning senior England caps.

Composed in possession and strong in the air and in the tackle, Tomkins took his game to a new level during the 2011/12 season, missing just two league matches and scoring four important goals.

With more than 50 Premier League appearances already under his belt, the centre-back began the 2012/13 campaign eager to stamp his mark on the top tier of English football.

5 JAMES TOMKINS

England international winger Matt Jarvis became West Ham United's club-record signing when he joined from Wolverhampton Wanderers in August 2012.

After being released by Millwall as a youngster, Jarvis quickly became a star with Gillingham as a teenager before joining Wolves in June 2007.

The wideman made his mark in the Premier League with a number of eye-catching displays, earning his first senior England cap in a 1-1 friendly international draw with Ghana at Wembley in March 2011.

Born: 22 May 1986, Middlesbrough, England

Position: Winger

Height: 1.70m

Former club: Wolverhampton Wanderers

International: England (1 cap)

MATT JARVIS 7

Born: 6 January 1989, Gateshead, England

Position: Striker

Height: 1.91m

Former club: Liverpool

International: England (7 caps, 2 goals)

Andy Carroll moved to West Ham United from Liverpool for the remainder of the 2012/13 Barclays Premier League campaign on 30 August 2012, with the Hammers having the option to complete a permanent deal for an undisclosed fee next summer.

Carroll, a powerful forward who is an outstanding header of the ball and blessed with superb technical ability, led the line for his country at EURO 2012, scoring in England's 3-2 group-stage victory over Sweden.

The 23-year-old initially made his name with Newcastle United, scoring on his first home start at St James' Park in a Premier League draw with West Ham in January 2009.

8 ANDY CARROLL

Big and powerful, Carlton Cole has led the line for West Ham United since joining the Club from Chelsea in the summer of 2006, scoring more than 50 goals in claret and blue.

The England international striker has finished as the Hammers' leading scorer in each of the previous four seasons, bagging 15 times as West Ham gained promotion back to the Barclays Premier League in 2011/12.

Cole completed a fine campaign by firing in the first goal in the 2-1 npower Championship Play-Off final victory over Blackpool at Wembley in May 2012.

Born: 12 October 1983, Croydon, England

Position: Centre forward

Height: 1.91m

Former club: Chelsea

International: England (7 caps)

CARLTON COLE 9

A versatile midfield player, Jack Collison has played all across the middle of the park since making his West Ham United debut at Arsenal on New Year's Day 2008.

After making his senior Wales debut at the age of 19, Collison has recovered from a serious knee injury to again become an influential player for both Club and country.

To prove that point, the popular player netted both vital goals in the Hammers' 2-0 npower Championship Play-Off semi-final first leg victory at Cardiff City in May 2012.

Born: 2 October 1988, Watford, England

Position: Midfielder

Height: 1.82m

Former club: None

International: Wales (11 caps)

JACK COLLISON 10

Born: 3 September 1987, Bamako, Mali

Height: 1.85m

Former club: FC Sochaux-Montbeliard

International caps: Mali (31 caps, 5 goals)

Quick and direct, Modibo Maiga joined West Ham United on a four-year contract after netting 24 league goals in two seasons for French Ligue 1 club FC Sochaux-Montbeliard.

After starting his career in his homeland of Mali, Maiga moved to Morocco before making his name playing for French side Le Mans UC72, where he lined up alongside Arsenal's Gervinho and Sunderland's Stephane Sessegnon.

Maiga has been a regular starter for Mali in recent years, appearing at the 2012 CAF Africa Cup of Nations.

11 MODIBO MAIGA

An outstanding talent, Ricardo Vaz Te arrived in English football at Bolton Wanderers at the age of 16 in 2003 and made 78 first-team appearances over seven seasons with the Trotters.

After a serious knee injury threatened his career, the Portuguese forward impressed for Scottish side Hibernian and Barnsley before joining West Ham United in January 2012.

Vaz Te made a sensational start to life in east London, scoring 12 goals in 18 games, including a memorable late winner in the npower Championship Play-Off final victory over Blackpool at Wembley.

Born: 1 October 1986, Lisbon, Portugal

Position: Forward/winger

Height: 1.88m

Former club: Barnsley

International: Portugal Under-23 (2 caps, 2 goals)

RICARDO VAZ TE 12

Highly-rated goalkeeper Stephen Henderson completed a permanent move to West Ham United in May 2012, having spent the previous two months on loan at the Boleyn Ground from then-npower Championship rivals Portsmouth.

A member of a goalkeeping family, Henderson began his career with Dublin-based Belvedere FC before moving to English football with Aston Villa in 2006.

After four years at Bristol City, the stopper impressed during an eight-month spell with Pompey before becoming a Hammer.

Born: 2 May 1988, Dublin, Republic of Ireland

Position: Goalkeeper

Height: 1.93m

Former club: Portsmouth

International: Republic of Ireland Under-21 (8 caps)

STEPHEN HENDERSON 13

Born: 27 November 1981, Oxford, England

Position: Left-back/left winger

Height: 1.78m

Former club: Bolton Wanderers

International: England B (1 cap)

Matt Taylor brought a wealth of experience to the Boleyn Ground when he joined West Ham United in the summer of 2011, as well as his famous left foot.

The scorer of spectacular goals during spells with Luton Town, Portsmouth and Bolton Wanderers, where he appeared in the UEFA Cup, Taylor was an important figure as the Hammers gained promotion from the npower Championship in 2011/12.

A versatile performer and likeable character, Taylor's raking pass set-up Carlton Cole for the opening goal of the 2-1 npower Championship Play-Off final victory over Blackpool at Wembley in May 2012.

14 MATT TAYLOR

The ever-popular Mark Noble capped an outstanding 2011/12 npower Championship season by being crowned Hammer of the Year for the first time.

The inspirational midfielder was a virtual ever-present as West Ham United won promotion back to the Barclays Premier League at the first attempt, scoring eight goals including seven successful penalties.

A former England Under-21 captain, Noble is still young enough to harbour realistic hopes of earning a senior call-up for his country in the future.

Born: 8 May 1987, Canning Town, England

Position: Central midfielder

Height: 1.77m

Former club: Ipswich Town (loan)

International: England Under-21 (20 caps, 3 goals)

MARK NOBLE 16

Born: 17 February 1986, Dublin, Republic of Ireland

Position: Right-back/defensive midfielder

Height: 1.8m

Former club: Bolton Wanderers

International: Republic of Ireland (3 caps)

After bursting into the Bolton Wanderers first team at the age of 18 in September 2004, Joey O'Brien was tipped for great things before his career was threatened by a serious knee injury.

The versatile Republic of Ireland international rebuilt his confidence and regained his fitness in time to earn a contract with West Ham United in the summer of 2011.

O'Brien's first season at the Boleyn Ground saw him make an impressive 32 npower Championship appearances, scoring an outstanding goal in the 4-0 victory at Watford in August 2011.

17 JOEY O'BRIEN

On 1 August 2012, James Collins signed a four-year contract on re-joining West Ham United from Aston Villa for an undisclosed fee, three years after leaving the Boleyn Ground for Villa Park.

Capped 39 times by his country, the popular centre-back was part of the West Ham side that completed a great escape from Premier League relegation in 2007, impressing the Boleyn Ground faithful with his power and commitment.

Collins began his career with Cardiff CIty, helping the Bluebirds to win promotion to the Championship in 2003 before spending four seasons with West Ham United between 2005 and 2009.

Born: 23 August 1983, Newport, Wales

Position: Centre-back

Height: 1.93m

Former club: Aston Villa

International: Wales (39 caps, 2 goals)

JAMES COLLINS 19

Born: 13 June 1981, Orsay, France

Position: Right-back

Height: 1.89m

Former club: Hamburger SV

International: Ivory Coast (35 caps)

Strong, powerful and direct, Guy Demel added great experience to the West Ham United squad when he arrived from German giants Hamburger SV in the summer of 2011.

A series of injuries slowed the Ivory Coast international's progress at the start of his first season in east London, but the right-back came back strongly in the New Year.

Demel ended the season by making ten starts in his maiden campaign with the Hammers, including all three npower Championship Play-Off fixtures.

20 GUY DEMEL

Born: 14 June 1987, Creteil, France

Position: Central midfielder

Height: 1.85m

Former club: Wigan Athletic

International: Senegal (12 caps)

A tall, athletic midfielder blessed with superb physical attributes, Mohamed Diame joined West Ham United from Wigan Athletic in the summer of 2012.

The Senegal international made his name playing for Spanish side Rayo Vallecano, being linked with moves to Real Madrid CF, Barcelona and Arsenal before joining Wigan in 2009.

After three fine seasons with the Latics, Diame was tempted to London, signing for the newly-promoted Hammers on a three-year contract.

21 MOHAMED DIAME

2006 FIFA World Cup runner-up and 2012 UEFA European Championship star Alou Diarra joined the Hammers on a three-year contract from Olympique Marseille for an undisclosed fee in August 2012.

Capped 44 times, Diarra has enjoyed a fine playing career, winning the French title twice, appearing in the UEFA Champions League nearly 30 times and captaining his country.

Born in the northern Paris suburb of Villepinte, the 6'3 tall defensive midfielder is known for his outstanding physical attributes and leadership abilities.

Born: 15 July 1981, Villepinte, France

Position: Defensive midfielder

Height: 1.9m

Former club: Olympique Marseille

International: France (44 caps)

ALOU DIARRA 23

Born: 24 May 1990, Woodford, England

Position: Centre-back/ right-back

Height: 1.91m

Former club: Bristol City (loan)

International: England Under-21 (1 cap)

A West Ham United Academy graduate, Jordan Spence has played for England at every age-group level, captaining his country and scoring the winning goal against Brazil at the 2007 FIFA Under-17 World Cup.

At club level, Spence was loaned to Leyton Orient and Scunthorpe United before making his Hammers' debut in the 1-1 Premier League draw with Manchester City on the final day of the 2009/10 season.

Either side of two loan spells at Bristol City, Spence returned to West Ham in April 2011 and featured in two Premier League matches.

27 JORDAN SPENCE

Switzerland Under-20 international Raphael Spiegel has represented his country at U17, U18, U19 and U20 level and is regarded as one of his country's outstanding prospects.

The 6'3 tall also made four appearances for Switzerland's U19s and travelled to the FIFA U17 World Cup finals in Nigeria in 2009.

Despite his tender years, Spiegel appeared 17 times for SC Bruhl SG in the Swiss Challenge League and in 41 games for Grasshopper Club's second team.

Born: 19 December 1992, Rüttenen, Switzerland

Position: Goalkeeper

Height: 1.96m

Former club: Grasshopper Club Zurich

International: Switzerland Under-20 (2 caps)

RAPHAEL SPIEGEL 30

Born: 18 May 1983, Bromley, England

Position: Midfielder

Height: 1.73m

Former club: Middlesbrough

International: England Under-21 (9 caps)

An all-action midfield player capable of filling a variety of roles, Gary O'Neil played an important part in West Ham United's promotion from the npower Championship in 2011/12.

After suffering a serious ankle injury just months after arriving at the club from Middlesbrough in January 2011, O'Neil fought back to fitness and form to score twice in 27 appearances as the Hammers went up.

Previously, the golf-mad midfielder had performed in the Premier League with aplomb with both Boro and Portsmouth and captained England at Under-21 level.

32 GARY O'NEIL

A versatile and composed defender blessed with great ability, Dan Potts has followed his famous father Steve through the ranks at the Academy of Football.

Potts was rewarded with a first professional contract and first-team debut in the same week in December 2011, impressing as West Ham United scored a 1-0 home npower Championship victory over Barnsley at the Boleyn Ground.

Already capped by England at Under-18 level, the teenager is looking to make his mark for both club and country over the coming years.

Born: 13 April 1994, Romford, England

Position: Defender

Height: 1.72m

Former club: None

International: England Under-18 (1 cap)

DAN POTTS 33

Matthias Fanimo came through the Academy ranks at West Ham United before signing his first professional contract with the club in the summer of 2011.

Fanimo made his first team debut for West Ham on 28 August 2012 against Crewe Alexandra, coming on as a 60th-minute substitute in a 2-0 Capital One Cup second-round victory at the Boleyn Ground.

The winger's promise has also been recognised at international level, where Fanimo has been capped by England at U16, U17, and U18 levels.

Born: 28 January 1994, Lambeth, England

Position: Winger

Height: 1.70m

Former club: None

International: England Under-18 (1 cap)

MATTHIAS FANIMO 40

Born: 18 August 1993, Swindon, England

Position: Midfielder

Height: 1.75m

Former club: AFC Wimbledon (loan)

International: England Under-18 (2 caps)

Capped by England at Under-18 level, Academy graduate George Moncur is a talented all-round midfield player who can tackle strongly and pass and shoot with either foot.

The son of former West Ham United favourite John Moncur, the youngster came through the ranks after joining the club at the age of 13.

Moncur's promise was rewarded with a first-team debut as a substitute in the Capital One Cup second-round victory over Crewe Alexandra on 28 August 2012.

42 GEORGE MONCUR

An outstanding young forward, Rob Hall joined West Ham United at the age of eight before coming through the ranks at the Academy of Football.

After a successful loan spell with Oxford United, Hall made his Hammers' debut in the 2-1 npower Championship defeat at Derby County on New Year's Eve 2011 and ended the 2011/12 season with four first-team appearances under his belt.

Hall has also been a regular for England at age-group level, winning the UEFA European Under-17 Championship in 2010 before reaching the semi-finals of the Under-19 version of the same competition in 2012.

Born: 20 October 1993, Aylesbury, England

Height: 1.73m

Former club: MK Dons (loan)

International caps: England Under-19 (4 caps, 1 goal)

ROB HALL 46

Hammers all over the World!

West Ham United has been represented by more than 100 players who were born outside the British Isles

Aside from the four home nations and Republic of Ireland, the Hammers have drawn players and managers from an amazing 47 different nations. From Argentina forward Carlos Tevez to Uruguayan wing-back Walter Lopez, West Ham's foreign legion has always done the club proud. In recent years, the Hammers have also employed its first foreign-born managers in Gianfranco Zola and Avram Grant, further enhancing the cosmopolitan reputation of a club born in the East End of London 1895.

NORTH AMERICA/CARIBBEAN (7)

Bermuda – Clyde Best

Canada – Alex Bunbury (born in British Guyana), Craig Forrest, Mickey Newman

Costa Rica – Paulo Wanchope

Jamaica – Jobi McAnuff, Tyrone Mears

Mexico – Pablo Barrera, Frank Burton (born in Luapanso, Mexico), Guillermo Franco

Trinidad & Tobago – Shaka Hislop

United States – Ian Feuer, John Harkes, Jonathan Spector

SOUTH AMERICA (6)

Argentina – Javier Mascherano, Mauricio Taricco, Lionel Scaloni, Carlos Tevez

Brazil – Araujo Ilan

Chile – Luis Jimenez, Javier Margas

Paraguay – Brian Montenegro

Peru – Nolberto Solano

Uruguay – Walter Lopez

EUROPE (21)

Belgium – Ruud Boffin, Francois van der Elst

Bulgaria – Svetoslav Todorov

Croatia – Slaven Bilic, Igor Stimac, Davor Suker,

Cyprus – Yilmaz Orhan

Czech Republic – Radoslav Kovac, Jan Lastuvka, Ludek Miklosko, Petr Mikolanda, Tomas Repka, Pavel Srnicek, Marek Stech

Denmark – Lars Jacobsen, Marc Rieper

Finland – Hannu Tihinen

France – Jeremie Aliadiere, Christian Bassila, David Bellion, Sebastien Carole, Edouard Cisse, Laurent Courtois, Alou Diarra, Julien Faubert, Marc Keller, Bernard Lama, Frederic Piquionne (born in New Caledonia), Sebastian Schemmel, Youssef Sofiane, David Terrier

Germany –Thomas Hitzlsperger, Savio Nsereko (born in Uganda),

Israel – Tal Ben Haim, Yossi Benayoun, Eyal Berkovic, Avram Grant (manager), Yaniv Katan

Italy – Alessandro Diamanti, Paolo Di Canio, David Di Michele, Gianfranco Zola (manager)

Hungary – Peter Kurucz

Netherlands – Ray Atteveld, Jeroen Boere, Marco Boogers

Norway – John Carew, Ragnvald Soma

Portugal – Paulo Alves, Luis Boa Morte, Dani Carvalho, Manuel da Costa (born in France), Paulo Futre, Hugo Porfirio, Ricardo Vaz Te

Romania – Ilie Dumitrescu, Florin Raducioiu

Slovakia – Vladimir Labant

Spain – Kepa Blanco, Diego Tristan

Sweden – Nicklas Alexandersson, Freddie Ljungberg,

Switzerland – Valon Behrami, Fabio Daprela

Ukraine – Sergei Rebrov

AUSTRALASIA (2)

Australia – Chris Coyne, Hayden Foxe, Richard Garcia, Sasa Ilic, Stan Lazaridis, Trent McClenahan, Steve Mautone, Lucas Neill, Robbie Slater, Dylan Tombides

New Zealand – Winston Reid

AFRICA (11)

Cameroon – Marc-Vivien Foe, Rigobert Song

DR Congo – Herita Ilunga

Egypt – Mido

Ghana – John Pantsil

Guinea – Titi Camara, Kaba Diawara

Ivory Coast – Samassi Abou, Guy Demel

Mali – Frederic Kanoute, Modibo Maiga

Nigeria – Ade Coker, Victor Obinna, Manny Omoyimni

Senegal – Demba Ba, Henri Camara, Mohamed Diame, Papa Bouba Diop, Abdoulaye Faye

Sierra Leone – Leroy Rosenior

South Africa – Benni McCarthy, Berry Nieuwenhuys

UNITED BY NUMBERS

A numerical look back at the history of the Hammers

1 West Ham United have won one major European trophy, lifting the European Cup Winners' Cup by defeating German side TSV 1860 Munich 2-0 at Wembley on 19 May 1965.

2 West Ham United are one of only two teams to score three goals in an FA Cup final and lose. The Hammers drew 3-3 with Liverpool in 2006 before being beaten on penalties. Bolton Wanderers are the other side to do so, losing 4-3 to Blackpool in 1953.

3 West Ham United are one of three clubs to appear in two League Cup finals and lose them both. Bolton Wanderers and Everton are the other two.

4 West Ham United have played at four different stadiums since the club's inception in 1895 – Hermit Road in Canning Town, Browning Road in East Ham, the Memorial Grounds in Plaistow and the Boleyn Ground in Upton Park.

West Ham United have been involved in three 5-5 draws in their history – at home to Aston Villa on 3 January 1931, at Newcastle United on 10 December 1960 and at Chelsea on 17 December 1966.

5

6 Bobby Moore's No6 shirt was retired in August 2008 to mark the 50th anniversary of the England great's West Ham United debut against Manchester United on 8 September 1958.

9 West Ham United's longest winning streak of league matches was the nine victories they recorded from 19 October and 14 December 1985.

6

10 West Ham United hold the record for the joint-biggest victory in the League Cup. The Hammers defeated Bury 10-0 in the second round on 25 October 1983. That result was matched by Liverpool against Fulham, also in the second round, on 23 September 1986.

13 West Ham United won a club-record 13 away league matches during the 2011/12 season, which ended with promotion to the Barclays Premier League.

14 West Ham United have had 14 full-time managers in the club's 112-year history.

West Ham United won a club-record 16 home league matches in succession between 30 August 1980 and 7 March 1981.

16

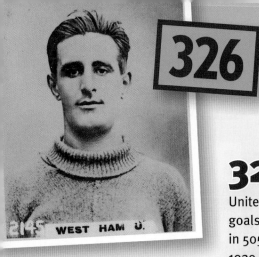

326

326 Vic Watson is West Ham United's all-time record goalscorer, netting 326 times in 505 appearances between 1920 and 1935.

19 West Ham United lost a club-record 19 consecutive away matches between 28 November 1959 and 15 October 1960.

27 West Ham United have gone 27 league matches without failing to score a goal on two occasions – between 22 January and 15 October 1927 and between 5 October 1957 and 4 April 1958.

708

42,322

A club-record 42,322 supporters watched West Ham United and Tottenham Hotspur draw 2-2 at the Boleyn Ground on 17 October 1970.

7,500,000

West Ham United paid a club-record £7,500,000 to sign Wales forward Craig Bellamy from Liverpool in July 2007.

29 West Ham United conceded just 29 league goals during the 1980/81 Division Two promotion season, a club-record low.

708 John Lyall took charge of West Ham United 708 times between 1974 and 1989, more than any other manager in the club's history.

18,000,000

The largest transfer fee West Ham United have ever received was the £18,000,000 Leeds United paid for England defender Rio Ferdinand in November 2000.

50 Vic Watson scored 50 goals in all competitions in 1929/30, a club record.

101 West Ham United scored a club-record 101 goals in securing the Division Two title in 1957/58.

Billy Bonds made a club-record 793 first-team appearances for West Ham United between 1967 and 1988.

793

793

1895 The year Thames Iron Works FC – West Ham United's predecessor – was founded by Arnold Hills.

18,000,000

WEST HAM FANS

Claret and Blue through and through

West Ham United fans showing their loyal support for the Hammers

Eat like a footballer

West Ham United team chef **Adam Viggars** with tips and recipes to help you to eat like a professional footballer.

West Ham United team chef **Adam Viggars** cooks for the first-team, Development Squad and Under-18s on a daily basis.

With input from manager Sam Allardyce and the Club's nutrition experts, the players stick to a strict healthy diet throughout the year to ensure they are in peak physical condition for training and matches. On a typical day, players should eat a balanced diet containing the right mix of proteins, carbohydrates, minerals and vitamins. At the same time, players should limit their intake of fatty foods.

Breakfast
Breakfast is an important meal, whether you are going to school or preparing for a morning training session, providing you with energy for the day ahead. Eating breakfast helps you to concentrate on the tasks in hand. As well as eating, it is important to take plenty of fluids on board to ensure you are properly hydrated. So, to kick-off your day, eat one of the following meals for your breakfast –

- Cereal with skimmed milk
- Toast with jam or honey (avoid fatty butter)
- Fresh fruit
- Yoghurt
- Orange juice, tea or coffee (with skimmed milk)

Lunch/pre-match meal
While footballers will eat three hours before a match – 12 noon for a 3pm kick-off – you also need to refuel at lunchtime by eating lunch. This meal should be high in carbohydrates, the fuel needed for your body to perform at the highest level, but low in fat, protein and fibre. To get you geared up for the afternoon or the big game, eat one of the following meals for your lunch/pre-match meal –

- Pasta with tomato sauce
- Grilled chicken breast or fish with boiled vegetables
- Fresh fruit

During the training session/match
You should not eat during a training session or match, but it is vitally important that you keep hydrated by drinking plenty of water and/or isotonic drinks. The body loses fluid by sweating and breathing heavily, so it is essential to remain hydrated to maintain your energy levels. It is also important to drink plenty of water immediately after the final whistle to replace lost fluids.

Post-match meal/dinner
Eating after a training session or match is very important as it helps your body to recover and replace lost nutrients – in particular the energy-storing molecule glycogen. So, you should eat a meal and drink fluids that are high in carbohydrates within an hour of finishing your exercise. Post-match meal ideas for you to try include –

- Grilled chicken or fish with rice or pasta
- Jacket potatoes (avoid fatty butter)
- Sandwiches (avoid fatty butter)
- Pizza
- Fresh fruit

Spaghetti Bolognese

- 2 tsp olive oil
- 1 garlic clove, crushed
- 1 medium onion, finely chopped
- 1 medium carrot, peeled and sliced
- 350g lean minced beef
- 1 cup of pre-sliced cremini mushrooms
- 1 tsp dried oregano
- 1 can crushed tomatoes
- 2 tsp Worcestershire sauce
- 1/4 cup skimmed milk
- 350g spaghetti

1. Heat olive oil in a large saucepan.
2. Add garlic, onions and carrots and stir until onions are softened.
3. Crumble in minced beef and cook until meat is browned.
4. Add mushrooms and oregano, and cook for a further two minutes.
5. Pour in tomatoes and add Worcestershire sauce and simmer for 25 minutes.
6. Pour in milk, stir well and simmer for a further ten minutes.
7. Meanwhile, boil pasta according to instructions on package.

Grilled Salmon and Boiled Vegetables

- 2 lemons, thinly sliced, plus 1 lemon cut into wedges for garnish
- 20-30 sprigs mixed fresh herbs, plus 2 tablespoons chopped, divided
- 1 garlic clove
- 1/4 teaspoon salt
- 1 tablespoon Dijon mustard
- 500g skinned salmon
- New potatoes
- Fresh broccoli, green beans and carrots

1. Pre-heat grill to medium-high.
2. Lay two pieces of foil on top of each other and place on a baking tray. Arrange lemon slices in two layers in the centre of the foil. Spread herbs over the lemons.
3. With the side of a chef's knife, mash garlic with salt to form a paste. Transfer to a small dish and stir in the Dijon mustard and remaining two tablespoons of chopped herbs. Spread the mixture over both sides of the salmon. Place the salmon on the herb sprigs.
4. Slide the foil and salmon off the baking tray onto the grill without disturbing the salmon-lemon stack. Cover the grill and cook until the salmon is opaque in the centre (around 20 to 25 minutes).
5. Meanwhile, boil new potatoes and, a short time later, fresh broccoli, green beans and carrots.
6. Wearing oven gloves, carefully transfer foil and salmon back onto the baking sheet. Cut the salmon into four portions and serve with lemon wedges (discard herb sprigs and lemon slices).

EASTENDERS

Cook your own East End Pie, Mash and Liquor!

No trip to West Ham United is complete without a meal of traditional East End Pie, Mash and Liquor!

The origins of this world-famous dish can be traced back as far as the 18th century, when 'Pie and Mash Houses' emerged as a popular place to buy a cheap and plentiful meal.

Back then, the pies were often filled with eels freshly caught in the nearby River Thames, due to their inexpensive price. The dish continued to be developed in the East End and is still eaten today at a wide variety of traditional Pie and Mash Shops, some of which even offer a delivery service.

The main dish today consists of pie, mash and liquor, with beef replacing eels in most cases. Liquor is green parsley gravy and is unique to Pie and Mash Shops, who all claim to have their very own secret recipe.

Eels continue to be an east London speciality sold in Pie and Mash Shops and are available in jellied or stewed form.

The East End favourite is now enjoyed all over the country, so why not ask a responsible adult to help you to create your very own traditional West Ham United dinner!

INGREDIENTS

For the pie filling
- 1 tbsp olive oil
- 1 onion, chopped
- 2 cloves garlic, finely chopped
- 450g/1lb minced beef steak or beef mince
- 1 tsp English mustard
- 1 tbsp tomato purée
- 1 beef stock cube
- vegetable oil
- 100ml/3½fl oz beef stock
- 2 tbsp plain flour
- salt and freshly ground black pepper

For the suet pastry
- 350g/12oz self-raising flour, plus extra for dusting
- 225g/8oz beef suet
- large knob of butter, softened, for greasing

For the pie crust
- 450g/1lb ready-made shortcrust pastry, for the top of the pie
- 1 free-range egg yolk, lightly beaten

For the mashed potatoes
- 2 large potatoes (preferably Rooster or Nadine), peeled, cut into chunks
- 100ml/3½fl oz hot milk
- knob of butter

For the parsley liquor
- 50g/2oz butter
- 50g/2oz cornflour
- 500ml/18fl oz chicken stock
- generous bunch parsley, leaves only, chopped
- 1-2 garlic cloves, roasted and puréed, to taste

PREPARATION METHOD

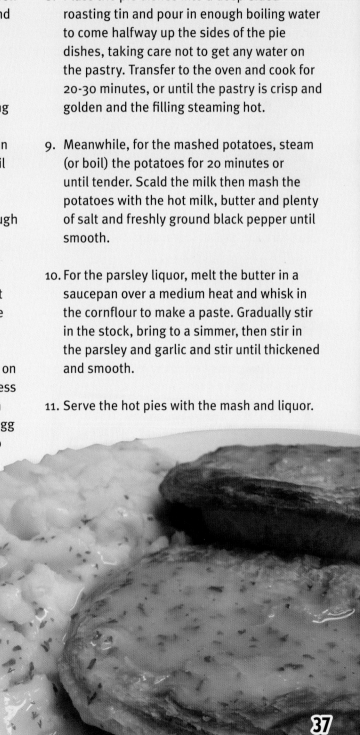

1. For the filling, heat the olive oil in a large frying pan over a medium heat and fry the onion and garlic for five minutes or until softened. Add the mince and cook for five minutes, stirring occasionally, or until browned and cooked through.

2. Stir in the rest of the filling ingredients, season with salt and freshly ground black pepper and set aside to cool.

3. Preheat the oven to 180C/350F/Gas 4.

4. For the suet pastry, sift the flour into a mixing bowl with the suet and season with salt and freshly ground black pepper. Gradually mix in about four tablespoons of cold water, or until you have a moist but firm dough.

5. On a lightly floured work surface roll the dough out to a 2mm thickness.

6. Generously butter two individual pie dishes then line each with the suet pastry, so that it covers the base and sides completely. Divide the filling mixture between the two dishes.

7. For the pie crust, roll out the shortcrust pastry on a lightly floured work surface to a 2mm thickness and use it to cover the two pies, pushing down the edges to seal. Brush generously with the egg yolk and make a hole in the middle of the lid to allow steam to escape.

8. Place the pie dishes into a deep-sided roasting tin and pour in enough boiling water to come halfway up the sides of the pie dishes, taking care not to get any water on the pastry. Transfer to the oven and cook for 20-30 minutes, or until the pastry is crisp and golden and the filling steaming hot.

9. Meanwhile, for the mashed potatoes, steam (or boil) the potatoes for 20 minutes or until tender. Scald the milk then mash the potatoes with the hot milk, butter and plenty of salt and freshly ground black pepper until smooth.

10. For the parsley liquor, melt the butter in a saucepan over a medium heat and whisk in the cornflour to make a paste. Gradually stir in the stock, bring to a simmer, then stir in the parsley and garlic and stir until thickened and smooth.

11. Serve the hot pies with the mash and liquor.

What's in a Kit?

West Ham United have worn dozens of kits since the Club was founded as Thames Ironworks FC back in 1895

Believe it or not, the Ironworks originally turned out in a dark blue kit similar to the present away strip being worn by the Hammers for the 2012/13 season. The Club adopted its famous claret and blue colours on a permanent basis in 1899 – the year before the modern-day West Ham United was formed – and have worn a variation on the original design ever since.

They Fly So High online museum curators and memorabilia collectors Steve Marsh and Stuart Allen have dug out five famous kits from the last 30 years and explain the stories behind them.

Boys of '86
When West Ham United finished in a club-record high league position of third in 1985/86, the players were wearing a strip manufactured by German company Adidas and sponsored by financial investment company AVCO. At the time of

1990-91 F.A. Cup 6th Round Everton

its introduction, some supporters felt the design was too different from the traditional claret and blue home kit, but it has since become one of the most-popular Hammers strips of all time! The shirt, which is still available as a retro item in the Club Stores, was also worn in the 1986/87 campaign.

Back to Bukta
After having been responsible for the Hammers kits of the mid-1970s, Bukta returned in 1989/90 to produce both the home and away kits which would be worn for two seasons, both of which were spent in the old Division Two. Just like the Adidas Boys of 86 strip, the strip – sponsored by BAC Windows – was synonymous with success as the Hammers ended the 1990/91 campaign by reaching the FA Cup semi-finals and being promoted to Division One.

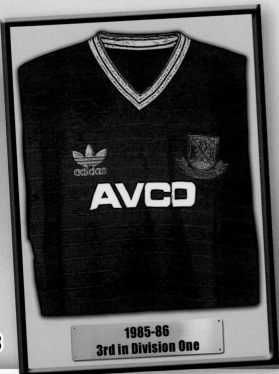

1985-86 3rd in Division One

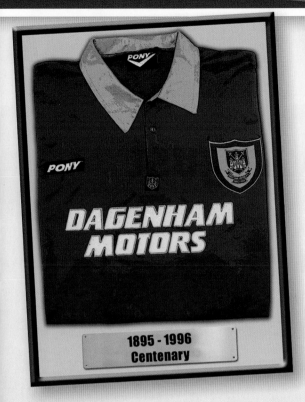

**1895 - 1996
Centenary**

Pony Express

The mid-1990s saw collars re-introduced on many football kits as was the fashion of the time. To celebrate West Ham United's centenary, American sportswear company Pony incorporated a bubbles pattern and the number 100 into their kit for the 1995/96 season. This shirt was worn for two seasons, with the highlight of its career being the 4-3 home Premier League win over Tottenham Hotspur in February 1997 that saw strikers John Hartson and Paul Kitson both score on their home debuts.

**2001 F.A. Cup 4th Round
Manchester United**

True Blue

Although it is now part of the regular cycle of colours for West Ham United's away kit, navy blue was a colour that had not been seen for many years until being reintroduced by Italian manufacturer Fila in 2000/01. This shirt has since become a best-seller as it was worn by the Hammers during their famous 1-0 FA Cup fourth-round win over Manchester United at Old Trafford in January 2001 – a tie that will forever be known for Paolo Di Canio scoring the winner as home goalkeeper Fabien Barthez cheekily appealed for a non-existent offside.

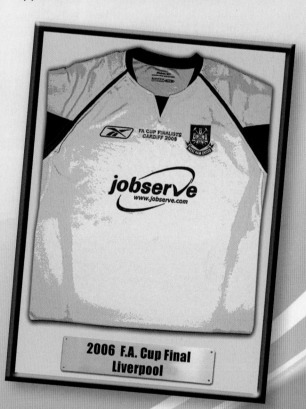

**2006 F.A. Cup Final
Liverpool**

Cup Final Fever

Designed by Bolton-based sportswear giant Reebok and sponsored by online recruitment company Jobserve, West Ham United wore this white away shirt on their return to the Premier League in 2005/06. That season, the Hammers finished ninth in the table while also going all the way to the FA Cup final. Wearing their white away shirt, West Ham produced a fine display at the Millennium Stadium, only to be edged out on penalties by Liverpool.

Pre-Season & August

West Ham United returned to pre-season training in July 2011 with a new manager in Sam Allardyce and a new captain in Kevin Nolan.

After a gruelling few days at Chadwell Heath, the Hammers spent a week at a training camp in Switzerland, where they also took part in the Uhren Cup tournament.

West Ham took on Swiss Super League sides FC Basel and BSC Young Boys, losing out 2-1 in both fixtures, before travelling to Denmark and beating FC Copenhagen 1-0.

Further warm-up matches against Wycombe Wanderers and Dagenham & Redbridge were followed by a 2-0 win over Spanish Primera Division side Real Zaragoza at the Boleyn Ground, with new signing Matt Taylor getting one of the goals.

The npower Championship season kicked-off on Sunday 7 August, but Cardiff City spoiled the party as Kenny Miller's last-minute goal condemned Big Sam's side to a 1-0 home defeat.

West Ham quickly got back on track, however, winning three straight away games at Doncaster Rovers, Watford and Nottingham Forest – equalling the number of away wins achieved during the previous two seasons combined.

At home, Leeds United secured a 2-2 draw courtesy of another last-gasp goal, while Aldershot Town caused an upset by winning 2-1 in a Carling Cup first-round tie that was forced to be re-arranged because of civil unrest in London.

Off the pitch, Big Sam had added to his squad by signing Abdoulaye Faye, George McCartney, Joey O'Brien, Guy Demel, Papa Bouba Diop, Henri Lansbury, Sam Baldock and John Carew, while Scott Parker was allowed to join Tottenham Hotspur on transfer deadline day.

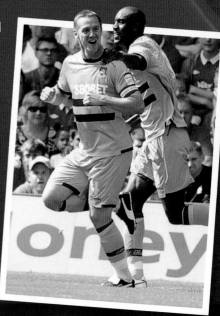

September & October

West Ham United continued their ascent of the npower Championship table as a thrilling 4-3 home win over Portsmouth broke Big Sam's Boleyn Ground duck on 10 September, with Henri Lansbury and Matt Taylor among the scorers.

A goalless draw at a thankfully peaceful Millwall was followed by a home win over Peterborough United, but another late goal – this time from former Hammer Lee Bowyer – saw Ipswich Town leave east London with all three points.

A busy October saw West Ham collect another three victories, including another Kevin Nolan-inspired away win at Brighton & Hove Albion and two pulsating home successes.

Sam Baldock was the main man of the month, scoring twice in both a 4-0 Boleyn Ground win over Blackpool and a 3-2 victory over big-spending Leicester City.

Norway international John Carew also netted against the Tangerines, while the re-born Julien Faubert collected his first goal of the campaign against the Foxes.

A haul of ten points from five matches in October saw Big Sam's side crack the automatic promotion places for the first time, rising to second in the standings behind leaders Southampton.

Indeed, the Saints were helped in their own quest for promotion by a narrow 1-0 win over the Hammers at St Mary's on 18 October, with centre-back Jos Hooiveld heading the all-important goal seconds before half-time.

Despite that setback, West Ham ended October just three points off the top of the table.

November & December

The Hammers consolidated their position in the automatic promotion places by compiling an unbeaten November that included outstanding away victories at Hull City, Coventry City and Middlesbrough.

However, the month began without any sign of the fireworks that were to follow with a goalless home draw with relegation-threatened Bristol City.

The Hammers rocketed back from that frustration by securing a 2-0 success at Hull on Guy Fawkes Night, with Sam Baldock and Jack Collison on target.

A hard-fought 2-1 win at Coventry followed, with Carlton Cole and Frederic Piquionne both having more than their fair share of fortune in finding the back of the net.

Kevin Nolan's 25-yard volley highlighted a 3-1 home success against Derby County before Piquionne and Cole combined again to shoot the Hammers to a fine win at Middlesbrough.

Unfortunately, December proved to be far less successful, with three defeats and just one victory – a 1-0 home success against Barnsley that was highlighted by a first-team debut for 17-year-old Dan Potts – from five matches.

Burnley stole a 2-1 win at the Boleyn Ground before Collison and Joey O'Brien were both sent-off in a forgettable 3-0 defeat at resurgent Reading.

Off the pitch, the players visited Richard House Children's Hospice in Beckton and King George Hospital in Ilford to distribute presents and spread some Christmas cheer.

On their return to action, the Hammers were held 1-1 at Birmingham City on Boxing Day before two goals in the opening ten minutes condemned Big Sam's men to a surprising 2-1 defeat at Derby County on New Year's Eve.

January & February

After a difficult December that saw them drop out of the automatic promotion places going into the New Year, West Ham United bounced back to winning ways with three straight npower Championship victories to open 2012.

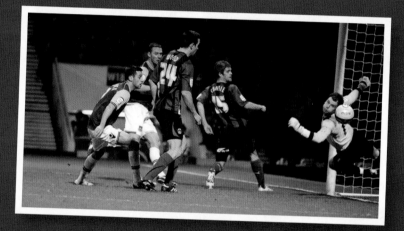

Coventry City were edged out 1-0 at the Boleyn Ground thanks to Kevin Nolan's header before Mark Noble's penalty secured three points by an identical scoreline at Portsmouth.

A 2-1 home win over Nottingham Forest took the Hammers to the top of the table on 21 January.

Aside from a disappointing 1-0 FA Cup with Budweiser third-round defeat at Sheffield Wednesday, the New Year had started in style.

January was closed out by a busy week of business in the transfer market as strikers Ricardo Vaz Te and Nicky Maynard were snapped up from Barnsley and Bristol City respectively, while young midfielder Ravel Morrison and American defender George John arrived from Manchester United and FC Dallas.

February was a month dominated by red cards as West Ham had a man sent-off in three consecutive league games.

Despite that hardship, Big Sam's men battled to a 2-1 home win over Millwall courtesy of Winston Reid's unstoppable winner and held Southampton to a 1-1 draw at the Boleyn Ground.

The best was yet to come as West Ham overcame the loss of Robert Green and the novelty of having midfielder Henri Lansbury in goal to score an amazing 4-1 win at Blackpool.

A frustrating goalless home draw with Crystal Palace to close out the shortest month of the year, however, was a sign of things to come.

March & April

As the npower Championship season approached its conclusion, West Ham United were faced with the prospect of playing 14 league matches over the final two months of the campaign.

March began with the Hammers in second place behind Southampton, but with in-form Reading breathing down their necks.

A fantastic 2-0 win at Carling Cup runners-up Cardiff City on 4 March appeared to allay fears of the Royals overhauling the Hammers, but a run of five consecutive draws then allowed Brian McDermott's side to take the initiative – and second place – by 17 March.

Against Watford, Doncaster Rovers and Middlesbrough at the Boleyn Ground, the Hammers were held to disappointing stalemates, while only a late header from loan signing Danny Collins snatched a share of the spoils at Leeds United.

A stirring comeback at Burnley secured a fifth successive draw, but even a 2-0 win at Peterborough United meant the Hammers would welcome Reading with the visitors a point and place above them in the table.

Carlton Cole's goal appeared to set West Ham on their way to a vital victory, but the Royals roared back to a 4-2 victory that all but secured their automatic promotion.

West Ham regrouped to thrash Barnsley 4-0 at Oakwell on Good Friday, but a 3-3 home draw with Birmingham City two days later further hindered their hopes of a top-two finish.

With January arrival Ricardo Vaz Te hitting a hat-trick, Brighton & Hove Albion were dismissed 6-0 at the Boleyn Ground, only for a 1-1 draw at Bristol City to leave the Hammers hoping for a Southampton slip-up in the final week of the season.

An Unforgettable Afternoon

Having finished third in the table, West Ham United went into a two-legged npower Championship Play-Off semi-final against Cardiff City. However, a potentially tricky tie proved anything but as the Hammers romped to a 5-0 aggregate victory.

The 2011/12 Play-Off final was a fantastic spectacle, from the sea of tangerine and claret and blue shirts that filled Wembley to the thrilling 90 minutes of football that further served to light up the Home of Football.

Blackpool should have been ahead, if not out of sight, within the opening 15 minutes. First, Robert Green pushed Stephen Dobbie's shot on to the post before Matt Phillips wasted two gilt-edged chances to put his side in front.

Having been let off the hook, West Ham went on the offensive and took the lead ten minutes before half-time when Carlton Cole latched on to Matt Taylor's diagonal pass before hooking expertly past Matt Gilks.

Ricardo Vaz Te would miss a decent opportunity to double the Hammers' advantage before the break, but the Portuguese forward would have better fortune a little over an hour later.

Into the second half and again Blackpool started the stronger, this time getting their reward when Phillips picked out Thomas Ince and the winger struck low past Green.

With both sides hunting for a winner, with Matt Taylor and Green denying Alex Baptiste and Dobbie either side of a fine save by Gilks from Cole.

As the game entered its final ten minutes, Kevin Nolan saw his goal-bound volley tipped on to the crossbar by Gilks.

Then, just three minutes from full-time, the captain's cross fell to Cole, who managed to prod the ball into the path of Vaz Te. The No 12 made no mistake, sending 40,000 West Ham fans into a state of ecstacy.

MYSTERY MAN

HI YOUTH ACADEMY MEMBERS!

CAN YOU GUESS WHO THE HIDDEN PLAYER IS BY ANSWERING THE THREE CLUES BELOW?

macron

BLAST FROM THE PAST

Clue 1: I am 25 years old.
Clue 2: I am a Portuguese International.
Clue 3: I scored the winning goal in the Championship Play-Off Final last season.

The mystery Hammer is

_____

Carlos Tevez is seen here slotting the ball under Manchester United's Edwin van der Sar to give West Ham a famous 1-0 win at Old Trafford... but can you answer these questions?

1. Can you name the year this took place? _____

2. What did this win mean for West Ham's season?
_____

3. Which fellow Argentine joined West Ham along with Tevez?
_____

BUBBLES' TRICKY TEASER

Which player received two red cards in his first three Premier League matches for West Ham in Autumn 2001?

_O_ _ _ _ _/_ _ _ K_

ANSWERS:

Blast from the Past:
1. Tevez scored the goal in the final game of the 2006/07 season.
2. The goal meant West Ham were safe from relegation to the Championship.
3. Javier Mascherano joined West Ham alongside Tevez.

Bubbles' Tricky Teaser:
Czech Republic International Tomas Repka was the player who was sent off twice in his first three Premier League games for West Ham.

Bubbles' Washing Line:
Shirt A belonged to (Matthew) Taylor, Shirt B belonged to (Jack) Collison, Shirt C belonged to Hammers Legend (Trevor) Brooking and Shirt D belonged to (James) Tomkins.

47

HAMMERABILIA

A special look back through the West Ham United memorabilia archive. West Ham United online museum They Fly So High curators Steve Marsh and Stuart Allen look examples from at the vast array of playground collectables produced over the past few decades.

Subbuteo

The first Subbuteo table football game was developed in 1947, just two years after the Second World War. The original sets included a piece of chalk to mark out a playing pitch on to an army blanket. The flat two dimensional players were made from cardboard standing on bases made from buttons weighed down with lead washers. There were two basic kits – red shirts with white shorts, and blue shirts with white shorts – and the goals were made with wire and paper nets.

SUBBUTEO Regd.

TABLE SOCCER .OO SCALE

MASSSTAB · ECHELLE · SCALA
(1:100)

TEAM

MANNSCHAFT · EQUIPE
SQUADRA · ELFTAL

WEST.HAM

by
SUBBUTEO SPORTS GAMES LTD.
TUNBRIDGE WELLS
KENT, ENGLAND

The year 1961 saw the first flick-to-kick 'OO' scale three-dimensional hand-painted figures on two-tone coloured bases we know today. Well over 500 million little plastic men have been manufactured since Subbuteo was launched.

Airfix

The name 'Airfix' will always be associated with the plastic model kit. Airfix is the oldest UK manufacturer of scale model kits and grew throughout the 1960s and 70s as the hobby became ever more popular. As well as military vehicles, ships, and aeroplanes they also produced soldiers, sailing ships, space rockets and much more including the 'Footballers Sport Series'. Each box contained 29 unpainted figures, including 24 players in various poses ready for you to paint in your favourite team colours, two coaches, two linesmen and a referee.

Action Man

For children growing up between the 1960s and 1980s, one toy stood head and shoulders above the rest – Action Man! The figure was first launched by the Leicestershire-based company Palitoy Ltd in 1966, based on the American Hasbro Toy Company's version named 'GI Joe'. Although usually associated with outfits dressing him as a soldier, sailor or pilot, the 'Famous Football Clubs' range launched in 1968 saw Action Man debut kitted out in a West Ham United strip, complete with a football, boots and a training jacket.

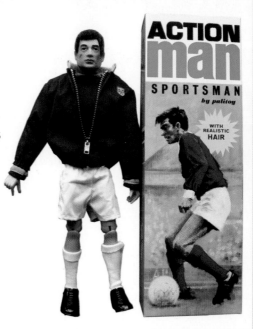

Trading Cards

Football cigarette cards were one of the first collectable items for football fans. However, with the banning of tobacco advertising, schoolchildren up and down the country are now much more likely to be swapping 'Match Attax' or 'Top Trump' trading cards or Panini stickers. Back in the late 1960s, it was FKS Publishers' 'Wonderful World of Soccer Stars' stickers that youngsters were collecting. The following decades saw Waddington Games Ltd's Top Trumps game become more popular, with each card featuring a range of statistics, enabling children to win cards from one another.

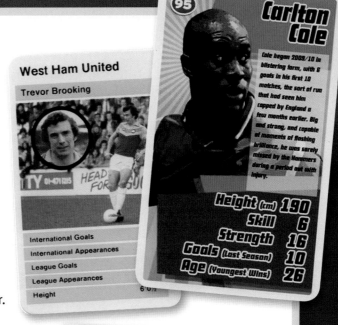

WEST HAM UNITED

A Week in the Life...

West Ham United captain Kevin Nolan takes you through a typical week as a West Ham United player

Kevin Nolan has been playing football at the highest level for more than a decade.

Aside from his talents, the West Ham United captain has had to ensure his body and mind are prepared for each and every match he plays in.

With that in mind, the No 4 keeps himself in shape physically and mentally seven-days-a-week, while he is at the training ground and while he is at home.

As captain, Nolan also has a host of other responsibilities to fulfil, from being interviewed by journalists to making sure any concerns his team-mates have are sorted out.

Here, the skipper gives you a unique insight into life as a professional footballer, on and off the pitch.

MONDAY

I normally arrive at Chadwell Heath at about 9am and have breakfast and sort out any issues or paperwork before getting down to work.

If we have played on the previous Saturday and do not have a midweek fixture to prepare for, Monday is a day of review and recovery.

We usually begin the week by holding a team meeting to discuss the weekend's match, where the manager and his staff go through the positives and negatives of our performance.

Physically, I will usually have a warm-down and treatment on any injuries before a light training session with the lads and some gym work.

After an energy-boosting lunch, I have a massage and deal with any other issues that the players might want to discuss with me. As captain, I will also talk to the manager.

I usually leave Chadwell Heath at around 4pm, but this depends on any of the regular charity or community events I or any of the other players often attend during the afternoon or evening.

TUESDAY

If we do not have a midweek fixture, Tuesday is what I would call a 'normal' day. We would have an activation session on the indoor pitch before going outside for a warm-up session led by our fitness coach.

Our training session will include a mixture of fitness and ball work, while we might do some tactical and team-shape drills if there is something pressing that we need to put right from the previous match.

A few of the lads might not train fully still this early in the week depending on injuries or whatever – but they or I would then do more gym work and one-to-one sessions with the medical staff.

For lunch, we will eat a lighter meal of something like chicken or fish with vegetables or pasta. During the meal, as we do all week, we also take on plenty of fluids to keep us hydrated.

By Tuesday, our performance analysts usually have footage of our next opponents, so

I will either sit down with them or take a DVD home to watch.

Again, the afternoon will be taken up by a massage or treatment, while this is also the day that we would fulfil any interview obligations for the website or matchday programme.

WEDNESDAY

Depending on the match schedule, Wednesday would normally be our day off.

Resting between matches is important and we are given instructions on what to do on our days off – it might be that we are told to rest completely, not do a lot of walking or anything strenuous or it could be that we are told to do certain exercises or maybe go swimming.

The lads who have not had as much playing time may come in to Chadwell Heath and do some light training and ball work and small-sided games to maintain their fitness levels.

Media-wise, Thursday is the day when I will write my Captain's Blog for the website and the manager and players will speak to the press ahead of Saturday's match.

My longest day of the week ends with a massage.

FRIDAY

We normally start Friday by holding our main pre-match team meeting where the manager and his staff give us an in-depth presentation on our opponents the following afternoon.

After activation and warm-up we go through our tactical drills on the pitch. This session is shorter than most as we obviously need to save our energy for the following day!

If our Saturday match is at home, we usually spend Friday night at home with our families, but sometimes we will head straight to a hotel after lunch to ensure we are completely focused and without distractions.

THURSDAY

With the matchday now approaching, Thursdays are much more focused on the opposition. After activation exercises, we will usually go through a mini-circuit training session before heading out on to the training pitch.

There, we go for a jog before going through some ball work, tactical sessions and working on set pieces, shooting and defensive work as little groups and as a team together.

The manager will normally ask the Under-18s and Development Squad players to line up as he expects our next opponents to play in terms of style and approach.

Thursday is normally our most intense and longest session of the week on the training pitch.

With 48 hours to go until kick-off, we have lunch and then will hold group or individual meetings with the manager or among ourselves to discuss anything that has come up or as preparation for the match in question.

Away matches mean travelling on Friday afternoon – by coach, train or plane – to arrive at our hotel late afternoon/early evening.

The evening would consist of a presentation ahead of the match, dinner and a massage to make sure those muscles are nicely stretched before going to bed!

Most of the lads take a laptop, iPad or books with them to help them to relax during the evening.

SATURDAY

Matchday! If we are playing at the Boleyn Ground, we arrive at the stadium just a little more than three hours before kick-off for our pre-match meal. We then have a team meeting and final presentation before getting changed, meeting the mascots and heading out to warm-up on the pitch.

After the manager's team talk, as captain, I lead the team out and meet the referee and my opposite number before we get down to business!

After the match, we eat a post-match meal high in carbohydrates to regain our energy levels before speaking to the press.

For away games, we get up at the team hotel at about 8am and have breakfast together before going for a walk. If the game is an evening kick-off, we might

hold a light training session before eating our lunch and having a sleep in the afternoon.

From then on, the routine in the same as for a home game, but of course we have to travel back to London afterwards, which may mean arriving home in the early hours of the morning.

SUNDAY

Depending on our fixture list, Sunday is usually a recovery day at Chadwell Heath.

We will come in and have treatment and a massage and may also have a light training session.

While we would all enjoy Sundays off to spend more time with our friends and families, we have to make sure we are in tip-top condition for every match and that means training at times when most people are not working.

Sacrifices need to be made, but we are happy to make them if it means we are in the best possible condition to represent West Ham United.

Next Big Things...

The West Ham United Academy of Football has produced dozens and dozens of top-class players, many of whom have gone on to represent their countries. From 1966 FIFA World Cup winners Bobby Moore, Geoff Hurst and Martin Peters through to Tony Cottee and Paul Ince to modern-day stars like Rio Ferdinand, Mark Noble and James Tomkins, the Hammers' production line has never stopped rolling. Under the expert eye of Academy Director Tony Carr MBE and his staff, West Ham's future continues to be in safe hands. Here, we meet five players who hope to be the next Moore, Ferdinand or Noble.

Former Australia Under-17 international centre forward Dylan Tombides was the second player to join West Ham United after being spotted while playing for the club's International Academy.

A prolific scorer for the Hammers' Under-18 and reserve teams, Tombides was promoted to the first-team squad during the 2010/11 season, being named as a substitute for the final Barclays Premier League fixture of the season.

A serious illness slowed the striker's progress during the 2011/12 campaign, but the popular Tombides is hoping to return to the pitch and start scoring goals again soon.

DYLAN TOMBIDES
**Born: 8 March 1994,
Perth, Australia
Position: Striker**

BLAIR TURGOTT
**Born: 22 May 1994,
London, England
Position: Winger**

Quick, direct and elusive, Blair Turgott has long been considered one of the brightest attacking prospects in English football.

Capable of playing on either wing or as a central attacking midfielder or forward, Turgott continued his improvement and development during the 2011/12 season, when he scored more than ten goals for the Under-18s and Development Squad.

Turgott has been a regular for England at age-group level, helping the Young Lions to reach the UEFA European Under-17 Championship semi-finals in 2011.

Sharp, clinical and with a low centre of gravity, Elliot Lee is never afraid to let fly with a shot, often being rewarded with another goal to add to his considerable tally.

The son of former West Ham United and England midfielder Robert Lee, the teenager has come through the ranks at the Academy of Football after joining the club as a schoolboy.

After a prolific 2011/12 campaign that saw him bag more than 20 goals for the Under-18s, Lee will be hoping to take the next step towards a first-team debut after becoming a full-time professional.

ELLIOT LEE

**Born: 16 December 1994,
Newcastle-Upon-Tyne, England
Position: Striker**

LEO CHAMBERS

**Born: 5 August 1995,
London, England
Position: Defender**

A ball-playing defender comfortable at either centre-back or right-back, Leo Chambers is another West Ham United Academy player who has represented England regularly at age-group level in recent years.

Quick, athletic and technically superb, Chambers captained England at Under-16 level before becoming a regular at Under-17 level during the 2011/12 season.

For the Hammers, the versatile defender was a regular in the Under-18s and forced his way into the Development Squad during the same campaign, despite being only a first-year scholar.

A box-to-box midfielder, Josh Cullen has been capped by England at Under-16 level, making his debut in a Victory Shield meeting with Wales in October 2011.

Blessed with good technique and boundless energy, Cullen became a first-year scholar for the 2011/12 season and will hope to follow in the footsteps of Academy graduate Mark Noble.

Such is his potential that Cullen was involved in the first-team pre-season fixture at Southend United in July 2012, just three months past his 16th birthday.

JOSH CULLEN

**Born: 7 April 1996,
London, England
Position: Midfielder**

PRE-SEASON ROUND-UP

Sam Allardyce's side contested ten matches in four different countries in preparation for the 2012/13 campaign

West Ham United travelled far and wide in preparation for the 2012/13 Barclays Premier League season.

Sam Allardyce took his players to Austria, Germany and Portugal as the Hammers prepared for life back in the top flight following their dramatic promotion at Wembley back in May. Pre-season began with a week-long training camp in the Styria region of south east Austria, where the players got fit in scorching temperatures.

After a productive week in the village of Bad Waltersdorf, West Ham played their first match, going down 3-1 to FK Austria Wien in the Austrian capital.

The Hammers returned to England to contest four domestic fixtures.

The players cycled to and from training in Austria

Blue Square Bet South outfit Boreham Wood gained a creditable 1-1 draw at Meadow Park before West Ham went up a gear at npower League Two club Southend United, where Nicky Maynard, Jordan Spence and Sam Baldock scored in a 3-0 victory played on a rain-soaked pitch.

A 1-0 defeat at Southend's divisional rivals Oxford United was followed by an entertaining 2-1 success at npower League One hopefuls Colchester United, with Maynard and Mark Noble on target.

Mark Noble was on target at Colchester United

The teams line up at FK Austria Wien

The Hammers' second foreign sojourn saw them head for eastern Germany for an intensive week-long stay featuring three games in the space of five days.

The trip opened with a 3-0 win at 3.Liga Rot-Weiß Erfurt, with Ricardo Vaz Te bagging two fine goals alongside an own-goal from Phil Ofosu-Ayeh.

A disappointing 3-1 defeat at Ipswich Town, Matt Taylor's goal aside, was followed by a much-improved performance at Portuguese UEFA Champions League qualifiers SC Braga.

West Ham were more than equal to their hosts at the unique Estadio Municipal and fully deserved the 1-1 draw secured through Winston Reid's 89th-minute finish.

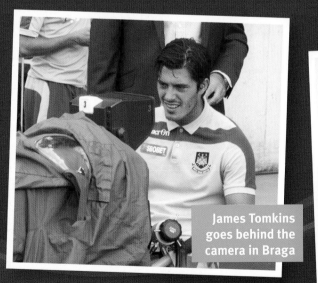

James Tomkins goes behind the camera in Braga

The Hammers training at the Estadio 1 Maio in Braga

That scoreline was reversed as West Ham took on Bundesliga 2 side Dynamo Dresden in front of more than 28,000 fans at the Glucksgas Stadion. The Hammers showed their spirit to battle back from two goals down draw their final game 2-2 at Energie Cottbus, with trialist Colin Kazim-Richards and Baldock getting the goals.

CALENDAR

	JANUARY	FEBRUARY	MARCH	APRIL	MAY	JUNE
1		David Sullivan (64)				
2					Stephen Henderson (25)	
3		Nigel Seidu (18)				
4				Josh Cullen (17)		
5						
6	Cheye Alexander (18), Andy Carroll (24)					
7						
8			Dylan Tombides (19)		Mark Noble (26), Gines Guzman Rosique (18)	
9						Wally Downes (52)
10						
11	Jake Larkins (19)					
12						
13				Dan Potts (19)	Nana Boakye-Yiadom (17)	Guy Demel (32)
14						Mohamed Diame (26)
15						
16						
17		Joey O'Brien (27)				
18					Gary O'Neil (29)	
19				Jussi Jaaskelainen (38)		
20					Lewis Page (17)	Thomas Gogo (17)
21		Taylor Tombides (17)				
22			Pelly Ruddock (19)		Blair Turgott (19), Matt Jarvis (27)	
23						
24						Kevin Nolan (31)
25						
26						
27						
28	Matthias Fanino (19), Matthias Fanimo (19)					
29	Jack Powell (19)		James Tomkins (24)	George McCartney (32)		
30						
31						

	JULY	AUGUST	SEPTEMBER	OCTOBER	NOVEMBER	DECEMBER
1				Ricardo Vaz Te (27), Ben Marlow (18)		
2				Jack Collison (25), Eoin Wearen (21)	Neil McDonald (48)	
3	Winston Reid (25)		Sebastian Lletget (21)			
4			Amos Nasha (18)			
5		Leo Chambers (18)				
6						
7			Kieran Bywater (18)	Josh Siafa (19)		
8			Martyn Margetson (42)			Frederic Piquionne (35)
9			David Gold (77)	Courtney Homans (18)		
10						
11	Taylor Miles (18)			Sam Baxter (19)		
12				Robert Girdlestone (17)	Carlton Cole (30)	
13						
14			Kieran Sadlier (19)			
15				Nathan Mavila (18)		
16						Elliot Lee (19)
17						
18		George Moncur (20)				
19				Sam Allardyce (59)		
20				Rob Hall (20)		
21			Kenzer Lee (20)			
22			Moses Makasi (18)		Dymon Labonne (19)	
23			Declan Hunt (20)	Callum Driver (21)	Dominic Vose (20)	Frazer Shaw (19)
24						
25						
26						
27					Matt Taylor (32)	
28	Paul McCallum (20)					
29						
30						
31						

Spot the Difference

Ricardo
Vaz Te